DATE DUE

DEMCO, INC. 38-3012

INSTRUMENTS *in* MUSIC

JAZZ AND BLUES

Roger Thomas

Heinemann Library
Des Plaines, Illinois

Designed by Susan Clarke
Printed in Hong Kong

02 01 00 99 98
10 9 8 7 6 5 4 3 2 1

Library of Congress Cataloging-in-Publication Data

Thomas, Roger, 1956-
    Jazz and blues / Roger Thomas.
        p.   cm. — (Instruments in music)
    Includes bibliographical references (p.) and index.
    Summary: Briefly discusses jazz and blues music and introduces some of their instruments, including saxophone, brass instruments, and piano.
    ISBN 1-57572-643-2 (lib. bdg.)
    1. Musical instruments—Juvenile literature. 2. Jazz—History and criticism—Juvenile literature. 3. Blues (Music)—History and criticism—Juvenile literature. [1. Musical instruments. 2. Jazz. 3. Blues (Music)] I. Title. II. Series.
    ML460.T423   1998
    784.165—dc21   97-49503
                                                                                          CIP
                                                                                      AC MN

Acknowledgements
The Publishers would like to thank the following for permission to reproduce photographs:
Trevor Clifford, pp.10 center, 22, 24 (Hertfordshire County Music Service), p.29 top left (Hill & Company), p.29 (Mo Clifton, Clifton Basses), pp.6, 8, 10 top and bottom, 29 top center, top right, bottom left and bottom right (John Myatt Brass and Woodwind); Dat's Jazz Picture Library, pp.14, 17, 20, 23, 25; Liz Eddison, p.12 right and middle, pp.12 left, 28 (Hobgoblin Music); Robert Ellis, p.18; Pictorial Press, p.21; Redferns, pp.13 bottom, 19, p.4 (Max Jones Files), pp.5, 13 top (Leon Morris), pp.16, 26, 27 (David Redfern); Sylvia Pitcher Photo Library, p.15; Zefa, p.7.

Cover photograph: Tony Stone/David Ball

Our thanks to Betty Root for her comments in the preparation of this book.

Every effort has been made to contact copyright holders of any material reproduced in this book. Any omissions will be rectified in subsequent printings if notice is given to the Publisher.

Any words appearing in bold, **like this,** are explained in the Glossary.

CONTENTS

INTRODUCTION

Jazz and blues music was started over a hundred years ago in the United States by African-Americans. Blues songs were often about hardship or love. Jazz music had a more lively sound and strong **rhythms**. It was often played by **marching bands** or at small concerts. Musicians often made up parts of the music as they played. This is called improvisation.

A jazz band playing an early style of jazz.

A contemporary jazz orchestra

A lot of jazz music is still played at small concerts. The music has grown very popular thoughout the world. Now much larger concerts also take place in big concert halls and at jazz festivals. The instruments are often amplified and the audience can be very large.

THE SAXOPHONE

A man named Antoine Sax invented the saxaphone in 1846. It is a **woodwind** instrument but is usually made of metal. A player plays it by blowing across the **reed** in the **mouthpiece**. She changes the **notes** by pressing **keys** which cover holes in the instrument. The bigger saxophones play lower notes and the smaller ones play higher notes.

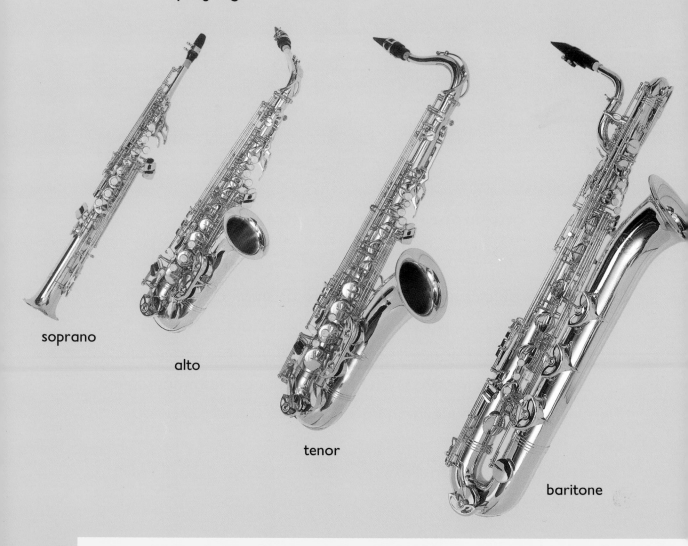

soprano

alto

tenor

baritone

There are soprano, alto, tenor, and baritone saxophones.

This saxophonist is playing a tenor saxophone.

A person who plays a saxophone is called a saxophonist. The saxophone was first played in **marching bands**. Now it is a very important instrument in jazz and blues music and is often used as a **lead instrument** in jazz.

THE CLARINET

A person who plays the clarinet is called a clarinetist. The clarinet is also a woodwind instrument. A clarinetist plays by blowing into a **mouthpiece** which has a **reed** in it. He changes the **notes** by pressing **keys** which cover holes in the instrument. There are several different sizes of clarinet. The bass clarinet plays the lowest notes. The clarinet and the bass clarinet are the two sizes most often used in jazz.

clarinet

bass clarinet

These are made of plastic.

8

The clarinet makes a soft, clear tone.

The clarinet was invented in the late 1700s. It was first used in **marching bands** and **classical music** over two hundred years ago. It is often used as a **lead instrument** in **traditional jazz**.

BRASS INSTRUMENTS

Brass instruments are made of curved metal tubes. The player makes a sound by blowing into a **mouthpiece**. The **notes** of trumpets, cornets, and flugelhorns are changed by pressing **valves** on the instrument. The valves change which tubes the player's breath goes into. Trombones usually have a slide instead of valves. This is an extra tube which the player moves in and out to change the notes.

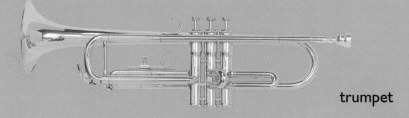

trumpet

These brass instruments are often used in jazz.

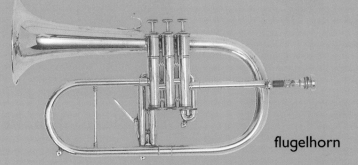

flugelhorn

trombone

The notes a trombone plays are an octave lower than a trumpet.

These brass instruments were first used in **marching bands** and orchestras. Trumpets have a bright sound and play high notes. This makes them good **lead instruments** in a jazz group. The trombone has a smoother sound and plays lower notes.

THE BANJO AND GUITAR

The banjo was developed in the United States over two hundred years ago from African string instruments. In **traditional jazz** bands the banjo is used to play **chords** which help keep the beat of the music. The banjo has a front like a drum, which makes the strings sound very loud. In modern jazz this part of the music is played on a guitar with metal strings.

banjo

archtop
guitar

acoustic
guitar with
bottleneck

The banjo and guitar are often used in jazz. Blues guitarists often use a bottleneck to give the notes a sliding sound.

Blues guitarists use guitars with steel strings too. They often play on their own and usually sing as well. Jazz guitarists often play **chords,** or they play **solos** using single notes. They usually do not sing while they play.

A traditional jazz banjo player and a modern jazz guitarist

BASS INSTRUMENTS

The double bass is used to play low **notes** in jazz music. The part is often very **rhythmic** and in time with the drums. The double bass has four thick strings. The player usually plucks them with the fingers of one hand. The notes are changed by holding down the strings on different parts of the **neck**. A person who plays one of these instruments is called a bassist.

This bassist is playing a double bass. It is the same as the double bass used in an orchestra.

This bassist is playing an electric bass guitar.

Some jazz bassists use an electric bass guitar. It is easier to carry than a double bass. It also plays low notes but has a brighter sound. Some players use one with no **frets**, which sounds more like a double bass. In **traditional jazz**, the bass part is sometimes played on a tuba or sousaphone. These are big **brass** instruments.

THE PIANO

The piano is a very important instrument in jazz and blues. It is either played **solo** or as part of a group. It is played in many different **styles** of jazz. A person who plays a piano is called a pianist.

This pianist is part of a jazz piano trio.

Blues pianists often play on their own.
Sometimes they also sing.

Blues piano music often sounds sad. This is because blues tunes and songs are usually about hardship or problems which have happened in the musician's life.

OTHER KEYBOARD INSTRUMENTS

Modern jazz players sometimes use **electric** or **electronic** keyboards, such as the electric piano. The electric piano is easy to carry to concerts. It must be played through an **amplifier**. It has a softer sound than an ordinary piano.

Playing the electric piano

An electronic organ usually has two sets of keys.

The electric organ has a big warm sound. Many players prefer to use old electric organs for this reason, even though there are now many newer kinds of electric or electronic keyboard instruments.

THE DRUM KIT

The jazz drummer usually keeps the **rhythm** and speed of the music steady. However, in modern jazz, he or she will often add lots of changes to the rhythm. The drums are played with sticks or with brushes made from wire or plastic. Some jazz drummers also use other percussion instruments, such as cowbells or woodblocks, to add different kinds of sounds to their playing.

This drummer is playing a modern jazz drum kit.

When jazz music first started, drum kits looked like this.

When musicians first started to play jazz, drum kits were often made up from drums and percussion instruments used in other kinds of music or from other countries. These could include **bass drums** and **snare drums** used by **marching bands** or **classical** orchestras, other drums from Africa or China, and Turkish and Chinese **cymbals**.

PERCUSSION

A large jazz group will sometimes have a percussionist as well as a drummer. The percussionist adds many extra **rhythms** and types of sound to the music. The sounds can include extra drum beats, woodblock sounds, and shaking and rattling sounds from tambourines and maracas.

All these percussion instruments can be used in jazz.

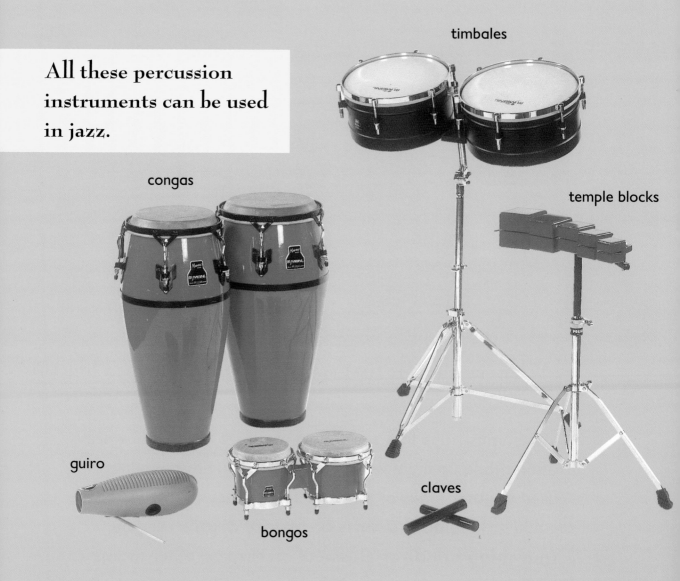

timbales

temple blocks

congas

guiro

bongos

claves

This Latin jazz percussionist is playing timbales and other percussion instruments.

There are different kinds of jazz from all over the world. Percussion is very important in **Latin jazz** and **Afro-jazz**. In some new jazz music, objects such as garbage cans, chains, and springs can be used as percussion.

THE VIBRAPHONE

Tuned percussion instruments have metal or wooden bars which are laid out like the **keys** on a piano. Unlike other percussion instruments, they can play lots of different **notes**. They are usually played with soft **mallets**. The player will often hold two mallets in each hand. The most popular tuned percussion instrument used in jazz is the vibraphone. It is usually played as a **lead instrument** in a small jazz group.

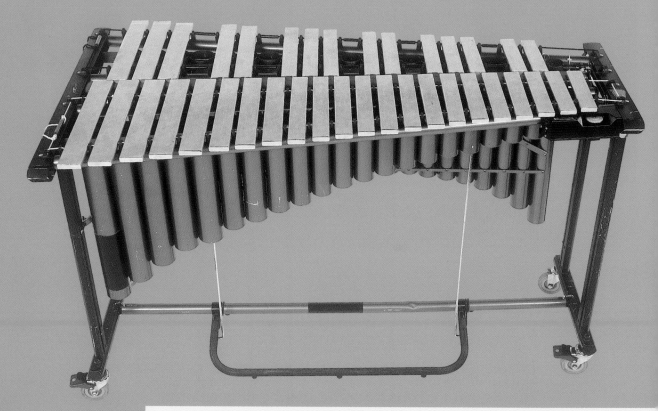

The vibraphone is a tuned percussion instrument sometimes heard in jazz music.

This musician is playing a vibraphone.

The bars on a vibraphone have tubes underneath them. Each tube has a small fan at the bottom. The fans are turned slowly by an electric motor. This gives the instrument a soft, echoing sound.

JAZZ AND BLUES SINGING

Jazz singing can be very exciting. It is usually performed by a **solo** singer with a band. Jazz singing can be happy, sad, exciting, or gentle. At times jazz singers sing made-up sounds instead of words. This is called scatting.

A jazz singer

This blues musician is singing while playing the guitar . He also has a harmonica.

Some blues singers sing with a band but many blues singers sing alone with a guitar or piano. Sometimes a singing blues guitarist will also play a harmonica to add instrumental solos to a song.

THE HARMONICA AND OTHER INSTRUMENTS

The harmonica was developed from a Chinese instrument called the sheng. The harmonica has metal **reeds** inside it which make a sound when the player blows into the instrument. It became popular in blues music as it is inexpensive, easy to carry, and can be played with a sad tone which suits the music's **style**.

The harmonica is widely used in blues music. A blues harmonica is often called a harp, although it has nothing in common with the string instrument of that name.

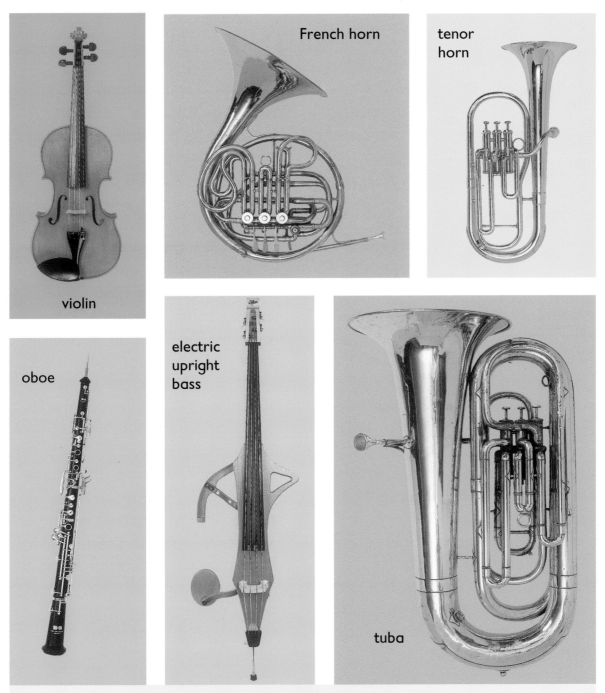

violin

French horn

tenor horn

oboe

electric upright bass

tuba

People who write or play jazz often like to bring new ideas to the music. One way of doing this is by playing or writing music for different instruments. The instruments on this page are unusual as jazz instruments but they have all been included in jazz bands.

GLOSSARY

Afro-jazz a type of jazz which uses ideas from African music

amplifier an electrical device which makes sound louder

bass drum a drum with a low sound

brass a hard metal used to make some wind instruments

chords several notes played at once

classical music traditional concert music started in Europe and often played by orchestras

cymbals two brass discs which are hit together or with a stick

electric an instrument which is playet through an amplifier

electronic a type of instrument which makes sounds using electrical current

frets strips of wire on the neck of guitars and banjos which the player holds the string against when playing notes

keys metal buttons on woodwind instruments which the player presses to change the notes

Latin jazz a type of jazz started in South America

lead instrument the instrument in a group which plays the main tune

mallets soft-headed sticks

marching bands military bands which usually play very rhythmic music

mouthpiece the part of a wind instrument which the player blows into

neck the long part of a stringed instrument with the strings stretched along it

notes musical sounds

octave the top and bottom notes of a musical scale

reed a thin piece of cane or metal in a mouthpiece which makes a sound when air is blown across it

rhythms patterns of notes in music

snare drums drums with wires underneath them which make a buzzing sound when the drums are hit

solo one musician playing

styles particular ways of playing music

traditional jazz a type of jazz which is like the earliest kind played

valves buttons on a brass instrument which help to change the notes

woodwind wind instruments other than brass

MORE BOOKS TO READ

Kliment, Bud. Billie Holiday: Black American of Achievement. New York: Chelsea House. 1992. An older reader can help you with this book.

Marks, Anthony & Rye, Howard. *Learn to Play Blues*. Tulsa, OK: EDC Publishing. 1995.

Raschka, Chris. *Charlie Parker Played Be Bop*. New York: Orchard Books. 1992.

Raschka, Chris. *Mysterious Thelonious*. New York: Orchard Books. 1992.

INDEX